# Journey Into The Unknown

### Finding The Courage To Move From Where You Are to Where God Wants You To Be

Sandie Heron

DAYELight
**PUBLISHERS**

ISBN: 978-1-949343-89-2 (paperback)

DISCLAIMER: The stories in this book reflect the author's recollection of events. Some names, locations, and identifying characteristics have been changed to protect the privacy of those depicted. Dialogue has been re-created from memory.

# Special Thanks

Thank you to everyone who has helped me along my life's journey. At every step of the way, God provides the right people and I am so thankful for everyone who has impacted my life in a positive way.

To my family and friends, I am grateful for your love and support. I especially want to thank Jheanell Ottey and Jodi-Ann Stephenson for assisting me with the editing process. Even though we were so far away from each other, your encouragement, especially during disheartening moments, made such a huge difference.

*"You call me out upon the waters,*
*the great unknown."*
*Oceans (Where Feet May Fail)*

**- Hillsong UNITED**

*BE BRAVE TO ANSWER THE CALL*

# *Table of Contents*

# *Introduction*

Many of us have a calling on our lives. Sometimes the calling comes in a gentle whisper and other times it is like a booming yell in our heads. No matter where we are, where we live, our circumstances, finances or the state of our personal relationships, there comes an appointed time in each of our lives when we will sense our call.

Something will nudge our spirits to tell us that there is more to life. There is more than our current jobs, the places we live and the situations that we may find ourselves in. We will feel it deep down inside of us. It will challenge us to not settle but will motivate us to shake off our fears and move out of our spaces of comfort and familiarity.

Letting go of areas in our lives that are like a "safe haven" can be one of the most difficult processes to go through. The fear is immense. We will wonder if we are thinking rationally or if we are about to make the right decision. It can feel heavily dreadful and if we are not careful, we risk remaining exactly where we are. I was at that place in my life some years ago.

I spent years working as a paralegal in Kingston, until one day I felt an inner prompting to leave my job. I believe I was receiving divine instructions to let go of some of the goals that I had already set, which included a degree I planned to pursue. I could not wrap my head around it, and at times, I questioned whether God was actually directing me.

I was fearful of making a mistake. I was afraid of potentially damaging my life and losing everything that I had worked hard for. Eventually, I found the courage to let everything go. I told myself that I would surrender, even if it meant that I would lose it all. When I got into that frame of mind, the instructions that I needed to move forward finally came. In this book, I recount the challenges I faced in trying to overcome people's opinions of my choices, my fears about whether or not I was making the right decisions, and the courage it took to leave my home in Jamaica to go and live in another country.

If you are at a point in your life where you feel stuck and unsure, I can relate because I was once there. I understand the crippling anxieties and fears. With this book, I want to show you that you are not alone. You do not have to give in to negative thoughts and self-doubt. There are many before you who have taken a similar journey and out of the challenges, they emerged victorious.

I hope my story will empower you to believe in yourself. The journey calls you as it called me, and it is worth responding to. Your soul will not be satisfied until you answer the call. You will know it when you feel it.

There are wonderful things in store for you, far more wonderful than you could ever ask for, think, or imagine.

I encourage you to start on your journey into the unknown.

Love,
Sandie

# CHAPTER 1

# *The Dilemma*

One Friday afternoon, I met with a staff member of the Law Faculty at the University of the West Indies to discuss my admission. This meeting was set up by my then employer. During the meeting, I remember clearly when he asked me if I wished to study law.

I remember sitting across from him in his office at the faculty on the first floor. He had an intent look on his face. His gaze was not intimidating, but it demanded an answer. It made me nervous because I was consciously following through with an idea that I was not totally comfortable with. I explained to him that I wished to develop my career. It was an insincere response. I felt as if I was reading from a script or rehearsing lines that someone had given to me.

The meeting went on. He and I spoke in more detail about my plans and what he thought was the best way forward. He offered study tips and other ways in which I could excel in the subject area. Then, he offered to take me on a tour of the faculty.

He showed me around some lecture theatres. At one stop, he told me I would be having most of my lectures in that room. Looking on, I considered myself tremendously blessed. There I was being given a VIP tour at the Faculty of Law. I thought that God must have had a hand in it.

After the meeting, I remember leaving with an increased sense of excitement about this wonderful opportunity, yet it felt somewhat strange. It felt strange that I was walking on the grounds of a place that I once believed God had told me not to go. That was my dilemma. Deep inside I felt, and dare I say knew, that I did not belong there, but I was not trusting my intuition.

CHAPTER 2

# This Thing Called Purpose

I surrendered my life to God in July 2011. It was at a small church close to where I lived in the Greater Portmore community in Saint Catherine. That day marked a complete turn-around for me. I was twenty-five years old at the time and was not truly at peace on the inside. I reached a point where I said, "no more." I wanted to quit doing life my way and I desperately wanted to find a way to fill the void widening within me. Nothing could erase the feelings of emptiness; not the arms of a lover, not parties, clothes, money or friends.

I started going to Fellowship Tabernacle and I began to learn about purpose. I learnt that each of us was uniquely designed by God to accomplish a specific task. It was the first message that really captivated my heart. "If everyone has a purpose, what is mine?" I wondered. I wanted to know the code that granted access to this locked away treasure. So, I began to pray about it.

> "If everyone has a purpose, what is mine?"

At that time, I was working as a paralegal at a small firm in Kingston. It was a path that I stumbled upon after finishing my first degree. The salary was not much, which was frustrating, as my student loan was outstanding, and I had other expenses to take care of as well.

On the advice of a friend, I applied for a more attractive position at a real estate company. The job description involved assisting the company's attorney, who had just been assigned additional duties. The attorney, Mr. Thomas, was easy to work with. He allowed me room to make mistakes without feeling incompetent. He did not believe in micromanaging and his approach was just what I needed to flourish. It was because of him and the easy flow of my job that I decided to pursue law. The thought had never crossed my mind before. Mr. Thomas thought it was a good idea too and encouraged it.

Back in church, I was still learning about purpose. I asked God to tell me what He wanted me to do. During that same period, my church announced an upcoming twenty-one days of prayer and fasting. I decided to participate in hopes of receiving a revelation concerning my purpose. I wanted guidance regarding major life decisions, such as my career path and personal life.

My pastor kept emphasising fasting and praying as an effective way to draw closer to God. He was right as I received confirmation concerning the areas that I prayed about. The revelations came through dreams and visions and the messages at church gave me even greater clarity. Some prophets also visited my church who spoke to me about my life. I had never met them before so I was convinced that their messages must really be from God.

One of the ministers had said to me, "The Lord says you are going to have your own talk show." It was hard to believe in that moment, but years later an opportunity arose for me to produce and host a radio programme. It is incredible how clearly we can hear the voice of God when we truly begin to seek Him. He really wants to help us when we need direction.

In relation to my career path, I sensed that God's answer to me was to focus on communications. He wanted me to focus on writing and producing videos. I spent a lot of time scribbling my thoughts and ideas on paper. My brain was always preoccupied with ideas of videos to produce or stories to write, no matter where I was. The whole process felt so natural to me. My interests that I thought were mere hobbies were placed within me to be used for His own purpose. This was the area that He wanted me to focus on, even though I could not foresee how any of these things could actually develop into a worthwhile career.

Being directed towards this career path was honestly a struggle because at the time I did not take it very seriously. Usually what we are called to do is not something we may readily accept. It may not be what we had in mind for ourselves and so personal sacrifices are required. We are all designed differently, so we are called to do different things. What we are designed to do will flow out of us naturally, like a bird that cannot help itself but to sing. You do not have to struggle to acquire what you already possess, but to use that talent for God comes with a sacrifice.

> We are all designed differently, so we are called to do different things.

When I received the revelations, I had a question, "How could I possibly make money from all the things that God was directing me to do?" I did not have any financial support from my family, and

I was living with a friend and her family at that time. In other words, I did not have the luxury of going off on a whim for the sake of passion and purpose. Nevertheless, I resolved to be obedient to God.

After the period of fasting ended, I enrolled in a voice and speech training, video production and editing course at a media institute in Kingston. One day my company's director saw the receipt after I had just finished paying for the course. After we had talked about what the receipt was for, he asked me how I would benefit. I was not sure of the benefit of it either, or what it would lead to, but I was going ahead with what I felt divinely led to do and what I really enjoyed.

After working at my day job, I would hurry to the institution for classes. It was an exciting experience and I met many other young people who shared the same passion. It felt right to be there every time I went. As I learnt about camera angles and audio editing, I remember feeling that the money I had paid was proving to be well worth it. I also questioned whether there was any point in going to school to study something that I had no real passion for, reading countless books and writing papers on topics that sparked nothing within me. So often we do things because they look good or because they have social merit but there is no real passion.

Imagine if everyone just moved in the direction that called them. I wonder what that would look like. I remember the joy I felt doing those courses. However, although I received training at the media institute, I did not immediately transition from my place of employment, due to my financial obligations and I also really enjoyed my job. I did, however, start a website and began writing on the side. Each week, I shared inspirational articles and invited other writers to share their stories as well. We documented the revelations we received, the lessons garnered from our experiences and shared them with others.

Many evenings after work I would lock myself in my office to enjoy the silence that remained after everyone had left for home. Those hours spent writing or filming gave me much more satisfaction than the eight hours spent around my desk during the day answering the telephone, organizing meetings, contacting various government agencies and clients.

Writing sparked a different kind of joy within me. When you experience that kind of joy, you know that you have connected with something deeper. When you do what you love, there is a deep part of you that comes alive. In those moments, I would go to a different place in my mind where nothing and no one else mattered. The universe appeared to stand still. My feelings of anxiety would settle, and in those moments, I felt so calm. Everything felt possible, and I felt nothing could hinder my dreams.

I was doing what I loved after work, yet I remained in that job for an additional three years. Occasionally, Mr. Thomas would meet with me to ask what my plans were for the future. At first, I went unnoticed, but as time progressed, other people in the company wondered if I planned to advance in my profession. The accountant who worked on the second floor told me to go back to school. At first, I told everyone that I had no real interest in studying law, but after a while it started to sound crazy. It felt like everyone was tugging at a raw emotion, picking at my fear of moving in the wrong direction.

Mr. Thomas left the real estate company and went on to start his own firm. I joined him and continued in my role as his paralegal and the dilemma also continued. How could a paralegal working in a law firm say that she had no real interest in a law career? Certainly, my earnings would have significantly increased had I chosen to pursue a law degree. After some time, my job as a paralegal did not make sense to me anymore. My resolve was strong at first but little by little my decision not to study law waned. I was losing my defences and I began to question myself. It was a difficult place to be.

Goi Nasu, a Japanese novelist said, "An entire sea of water can't sink a ship unless it gets inside the ship." Take a moment to imagine that ship sailing smoothly on a vast expanse of water. It appears untouchable, but this is only so, if there is no damaged area on that ship that will allow water to get in. In the same way, we will face many difficulties, if we allow the negativity and doubts of others to start influencing our own

> It takes work to control the mind and become our own best friend.

thoughts. Our minds also can be our harshest critics. It takes work to control the mind and become our own best friend.

People will not readily understand the things that you do. One advice I would give to my younger self is to know that it is okay if people do not understand the direction your life takes. The fact that they do not understand does not diminish the power of what you carry.

As much as I wanted to be obedient to God, I could not help but question Him. I even felt foolish. I really do believe that some of us are pulled from the crowd by God and it can make us look foolish, at least it looks that way at first, until things start to come together.

CHAPTER 3

# *God Speaks Through Dreams*

Dreams are one of the ways through which God communicates with us. It is a mysterious form of communication from the spiritual to the physical realm. We have to be alert to hear when He speaks to us, especially regarding the issues we have been praying about or in relation to problematic areas of our lives.

We do not have dreams simply because we watched a scary movie just before bed or ate late at night. Dreams link us to unearthly spaces in our subconscious. I know this because God always speaks to me through dreams. It may sound strange if you do not believe in supernatural ideologies and I understand because I also did not embrace them at first. Even now, there are times when I question what I see and at times I get terrified. If I receive a warning about someone close to me or a new venture I want to embark on, I sometimes become suspicious.

I was forced to believe what I saw, however, when some of my dreams started to manifest. When what you see or sense in the spirit realm starts to show up in your life, you must pay close attention. I believe God trains us to increase our levels of trust in Him. For example, you may have a dream about a friend who you have not heard from in a while, and later that day, you receive a text message from that friend or see a post about them online. Coincidence? I think not. Something is bidding you to pay attention, and as you start to take note of the small things, the language of dreams will develop.

In July 2016, I had two dreams that left me feeling quite uneasy. In the first dream my employer, Mr. Thomas, appeared and told me that I was at my job for too long and I should move on. I asked him, "What will I do?" He suggested that I apply to a local television company where they would give me lots of scripts and I could focus on what I love to do. In the same dream, I envisioned leaving Jamaica to live abroad.

I considered the meaning of the dream and admittedly felt a little suspicious. I became anxious and self-aware whenever I entered my office. I walked in and looked around as if there was something hidden for me to uncover. I could not share with my co-workers what I was experiencing so I kept it in the secrecy of my thoughts. Dreams take us to a place of intimacy with God. Sometimes what we see in dreams can be strange or frightening, so we are reluctant to talk about them. Consider yourself blessed if you have a close friend you can share with. The only action I was able to take was to pray and trust that I would later understand what the dream meant.

I tried hard to forget about the first weird dream but a month later, I had another. This time, I knew that I needed to pay attention because the second dream was a repetition of the one that I had before. Dreams come to uncover hidden things and to open our eyes to what we would never even consider. Usually, the spirit realm is signaling us, telling us that there is something that requires our attention, especially if there is repetition. It is telling us that there is something we are overlooking. The truth is, we do not always catch the revelation at first, hence, the need for it to be repeated. I am one of those people who learn from repetition.

In the second dream, I saw a colleague, who was a close friend of Mr. Thomas. She told me that I should apply for another job and to give it to her as a Christmas present. *"Dweet enuh, Sandie! Dweet enuh!"* (Jamaican patois for, "Do it, Sandie! Do it!") she pleaded. There was such urgency and seriousness in her voice. She spoke as if it was something that I absolutely needed to do and within a particular time. In reality, this colleague and I did not have that kind of relationship. We never discussed personal matters or my plans concerning work, so I was surprised to receive such an instruction from her.

Again, I felt uncomfortable. That day at work felt unusual. My office felt smaller, like it had shrunken overnight. I felt tall enough to touch the roof. I could see my desk, my chair, the two paintings hanging on the wall, the vase sitting in the corner and the grout between the tiles on the floor. It was like watching a movie that I was no longer a part of. It felt like I had stepped out of the picture and was just a mere observer. Whenever I feel that way, I know it is time for me to move on. Yet, I could not help but wonder if God was instructing me to leave my job. I was unsure. I wondered why He would tell me to leave and what I would do after resigning.

I decided to act on my instinct and reached out to a friend of mine who worked in media. I thought I would ask her for a connection to someone who worked at the television station I saw in my dream, so I could send in my application. If I was accepted, I planned to resign from the firm and start working in media. I had confidence that I would be successful too. Interestingly, during the same period, Mr.

Thomas met with me to discuss my future. He had been patient with me in all the years I worked with him and wanted to know why I would not pursue further studies. He expressed his thought that I was limiting myself and told me that I could achieve more. He mentioned that studying law would be beneficial, even to my passion for media, as people would take my platform more seriously.

Some weeks had passed since I received the dreams to leave my place of employment. I had a deep desire to continue to obey God, but I felt stuck. To make matters worse, after several interviews at the television station, I heard nothing. I felt stuck in my job and I felt stuck in my life. I watched as other persons who were about my age joined the firm in senior positions. This was not because they were more experienced than me but because they were more academically qualified. At first, it was not a bother but as I became more aware, I started to wrestle with myself internally. I wondered if I had been sleeping all those years I worked in the firm. At that point, I did not know God's expectations because I had been waiting and I did not think that I received any real instructions about what to do.

I thought I was foolish to trust my dreams. My belief that dreams come from God wavered. "How can one be sure that any dream is from God?" I wondered. It was getting harder by the day to keep believing. My self-confidence also started to diminish. I had a hard time looking Mr. Thomas in the eyes because I feared being judged. There was a part of me that still wanted approval from others, especially those in authority. I had not yet overthrown that giant.

> "How can one be sure that any dream is from God?"

On our journeys we must decide whose approval matters more. Is our need for God's approval greater than our need for the approval of others? Constantly seeking validation from the people around us can prove to be harmful because it can prevent us from doing the right thing and living in our truths. It is one of the fastest routes to self-betrayal.

I was confronted with a double reality. In the physical realm, Mr. Thomas offered to assist me with advancing my qualifications. He was sharing with me opportunities to progress in the firm and it all sounded great. However, in my dream the same person was telling me that it was time for me to go. I was confused. It is said that confusion is not of God, still when we reach a crossroads in our lives, it can be challenging to decide what action to take.

Have you ever had one of those moments where you found it hard to figure things out? I was right there, praying to be led on the right path but I felt conflicted because of what was happening in my dreams, versus what was happening in real life. I wanted to please others and I really wanted to feel as if I was progressing in my career, so I went ahead and applied for the law degree programme. I had half-hoped that somehow I would not get through but I was accepted.

We are not always blocked from walking away from the will of God. He will warn us but eventually we will be left to make our own decisions and go in the direction we choose. Sadly, it is only after some of us face the consequences of our stubbornness that we start to fully realise why we were being steered away from that path in the first place.

I was accepted into the degree programme and Mr. Thomas was happy for me. He circulated an email to inform all our work colleagues that I had been accepted and asked that everyone congratulate me. I really did not want everyone to know because I was not sure that I was making the right decision.

One day, someone called from a realtors' office that we worked closely with to congratulate me. She exclaimed that I could finish up studying and become a partner at the firm. It made me chuckle. The uneasiness that overtook me became hard to ignore. I tried to tell myself that I did a good thing and I was happy. You will find that you lie to yourself when you go down a path that is not meant for you. We are free to choose but we know instinctively when we have chosen wrong.

Some say we know in our hearts when we find the path that is meant for us. While this is true for many, some of us still struggle to find exactly what that right path is. I tried to convince myself that I had made the right choice. I told myself that I was advancing my personal and professional life, but I did not feel inner peace concerning my decision. I told myself that this was the best decision and that it was a way for me to climb the social ladder. I was not prepared, however, for the misery that would soon follow.

CHAPTER 4

# *The Pain of Making Bad Decisions*

Sometimes I go down the wrong path without realising until later. I then end up having to do a course correction with some uncomfortable situations to resolve. I hate it. I have always wished I could get it right the first time, but the truth is, we are imperfect and bound to make wrong decisions. I am truly grateful for God's grace that remains with us, even when we veer off course.

There are imperfect people, even in the Bible. Take Jonah for example. He was a prophet in the Hebrew Bible who was instructed by God to go to a city called Nineveh to deliver an urgent message to the people. God wanted him to warn them that unless they changed their wicked ways, He would severely punish them. Instead, Jonah disobeyed God and boarded a ship that was sailing in the opposite direction to another city called Tarshish. Jonah thought he was safe, but the Lord sent a great wind on the sea, that caused a violent storm which threatened to destroy the very ship that Jonah was in. The sailors wondered what the cause for their misfortune was and realised it was because Jonah was with them. They eventually threw him overboard (See Jonah 1:1-16).

Jonah, not wanting to go to the place where God was sending him, resonates with those of us who are hesitant to follow God's leading. Some of us, in our own wisdom, do not think that people who live in certain places are deserving of God's grace. We shy away and assume the worst about them, but God knows their hearts. Jonah's story is so powerful because it shows us how our disobedience can actually affect what God has in store for other people. It can also cause harm to others, as with the sailors, when we walk out of alignment with the will of God.

There is providence where God calls us. Going where He calls us does not always feel perfect, but His protection and provision are there. There are miracles and wonders where God calls us. In this place, at the right time,

> There are miracles and wonders where God calls us. In this place, at the right time, God always allows us to meet the right people and we access opportunities that are above and beyond what we could have even imagined.

God always allows us to meet the right people and we access opportunities that are above and beyond what we could have even imagined. It is then that we get a glimpse of God's plan for our lives and we start to understand everything that we went through that brought us to this place. A feeling of fulfilment comes and then we are sure that we are right where we are meant to be.

After Jonah was thrown overboard, the Lord provided a huge fish to swallow him. He spent three days and three nights in the belly of that fish and while he was in that dark place, he asked for God's forgiveness and decided to make a course correction. After he prayed the Lord commanded the fish, and it vomited him onto dry land (See Jonah 2:1-10).

God instructed Jonah once again to go to Nineveh to deliver His message and he obeyed (See Jonah 3:1-3). He preached to the people of Nineveh and they believed God's message and repented. Even the King of the city issued a proclamation that everyone should fast and pray to God for forgiveness. When God saw what they did and how they turned from their evil ways, He relented and did not bring on them the destruction He had threatened (See Jonah 3:10).

Many people were saved because of Jonah's obedience. There are people waiting on our obedience too. They are waiting on us to write a book, to film a movie, to open a restaurant, to defend them in a courtroom, to sing a soul-stirring song, to bring life back into their favourite sport, to deliver a prophetic word from God or simply to be their friend in a foreign country. We are the perfect candidates for what God has called us to do, even if we do not always know it.

> We are the perfect candidates for what God has called us to do, even if we do not always know it.

Like Jonah, I have found myself in the metaphoric belly of the great fish more than once. The fish's belly is that place of sadness, regret, and absolute disappointment before God. The decision to pursue that course of study brought about one of those times in my life. I can therefore, relate to Jonah's dilemma, and perhaps you can too.

CHAPTER 5

# When You Know Something Doesn't Feel Right

I recall the day I stood in line at the university to pay my first semester's tuition. Looking at my school identification card and seeing my photograph, it all looked good, but something was out of place and I could not shake the feeling.

Around that same time, I was producing and hosting City Beat, a programme on Roots 96.1FM, a local radio station in Kingston. The week before the start of my classes, one of the producers at the radio station asked me to conduct an interview with a friend of hers who was interested in telling his story. I arranged for him to meet me at my office and when we met, coincidentally, he spoke to me about purpose.

Denny chronicled his journey of applying to study engineering at the University of Technology and he explained how hard it was for him to continue the programme. It was hard for him because he had a passion for music. When he spoke about it, there was sheer excitement in his eyes. There was a certain spark about him. His friends and family encouraged him to continue but he chose to withdraw from the programme and pursue his passion for music.

There are people who are stuck in professions they hate but they choose to stay because the job is reputable or because they make a lot of money. There are others too who are just doing what they have to do. While I understand this, I don't think this is what our personal journeys should be about. We do not get to spend eternity on Earth, and I believe nothing brings greater fulfilment than tapping into our purpose, guided by our passion.

Denny was one of those people brave enough to tap in and when he spoke to me, I could relate on a deep and knowing level. I struggled to hold back tears as I spoke to him, and inside I wondered if God was trying yet again to tell me something. What he was sharing sounded much like my own situation, except he had already gone through the process and I was only just getting started. I told my story to Denny and shared with him how I was feeling at the time. In retrospect, I realised his story contained both a lesson and a caution.

My friend, you must pay attention to the signs that God shows you. We pray and wonder if God hears us, but we are not always open to the ways that He sends us an answer. Many people look for answers from their pastors or some spiritual gurus, but the answers we need often present themselves in other ways.

Life is dynamic. How I receive messages may not be how you receive them. While I may get dreams, your prayers may be answered in a book you read, a chance word you hear in a conversation, a song on the radio or some other thing that holds meaning for you. If you pay attention, you will see what God is trying to show you and you will realise that you are not left to figure things out on your own.

After that meeting with Denny, I wondered if I should go to my soon commencing classes. I wondered if I should cancel the tuition cheque, but I figured I was being ridiculous. I wondered too if God was speaking to me or if it was fear trying to keep me away from elevating myself.

The questions in my head were many. Believe it or not, after all that conundrum, I found myself sitting in the lecture theatre at the law faculty of the University of the West Indies for my first day of school.

CHAPTER 6

# *Removing the Facades*

The sting of disobedience is painful. It is that moment when you know without a doubt that you messed up. You do not feel at peace with yourself and are so far gone that you do not know what to do anymore. That uneasy feeling is what I felt during the months of my first semester. Like a scratched record, I kept hearing messages about disobedience. They were on the radio, in books, on social media and every time I heard or saw them, I felt like they were directed to me.

I felt so deeply that I had disappointed God and I prayed and asked for His mercy. I was most afraid that I would walk completely out of His will and cancel the purpose that He had for my life. Everyone at work knew that I had started school. All the conversations that I had with work colleagues included what I was doing there. I would hear, "Sandie, how is it going?" or "You are going to do well," or "You can get qualified and eventually open your own firm or become a partner." My heart did not leap at their comments as it did when I was excited about a new venture. My heart was just not in it.

I just wanted to write. I wanted to write books, stories, and articles. I wanted to be free with my

46

creativity. I wanted to travel to all the places I saw on television and in my dreams. I wanted to meet people, capture their stories, and share those stories with others. That was what my inner being craved, but I always smiled with my work colleagues. I told them it was going well and that the courses were easy for me because I was already familiar with some of the material. I was lying through my teeth and I knew it.

> Each time you move in a direction that you know you are not meant to go, you go against your intuition.

Each time you move in a direction that you know you are not meant to go, you go against your intuition. After a while, I got sick of it. I got sick of saying that it was going well when it was not true. I felt like I betrayed myself. I had gone ahead and done the opposite of what my spirit prompted me to do. I put on a show and pretended for the approval of people and risked losing the approval of God.

The hardest decision I made was to be truthful, not only to others but more so to myself. I decided to put everything on the line. After years of people telling me what to do and who they thought I should be, after years of me doing my best to be accepted by others - for the first time in my life, I was going to be true to myself, despite all it could cost me.

About two or three months into the school year, I decided I would not continue beyond the first semester. I was sure then that all I wanted to do was to submit to the journey that called me first.

CHAPTER 7

# Moment of Truth

One dreaded morning, in a staff meeting a few weeks before my final exams, Mr. Thomas asked about school. I could only muffle an answer and slightly shrug my shoulders. He read my response and asked if I was enjoying it and I told him I was not. It was the first time I had told the truth in months. I had to remind myself to breathe.

We continued the meeting discussing other things related to clients and some cases. I tried to remain focused, but I was unnerved by what I had done. When the meeting ended, I made my way out of the building, sat in my car, and cried. I felt foolish and thought about what others would say about me. Why do we worry so much about the opinions of others? Pleasing people is a sure killer of dreams, but I was not experienced enough to know this at the time.

> Why do we worry so much about the opinions of others? Pleasing people is a sure killer of dreams.

After that episode, I regained my composure and headed back to my office. As soon as I returned to my desk, I received a Facebook notification - a girl

I had worked with some years before tagged me in a post. When I saw it on my phone, I read it so that I could take my mind off the meeting. The post was about ego and love and specifically about the battle between them. I wondered what it meant. I did not want to misinterpret the post, so I asked her if there was something for me to take from it. She told me, *"You came to mind when I was writing about when times are hard, EGO dies ... that is the best I can say as to why."*

I asked her to explain the ego to me. She wrote back, *"Whatever we focus on for the purpose of image to others and ourselves that usually looks good on the outside but has no substance and usually takes us away from our life's purpose or higher self."* I then understood the message. This is another example of there being signs all around us. Things do not happen just by chance. If we pay attention, we will recognise the signs when they come to help us.

We get help and guidance as we set out on our respective journeys to find higher meaning for our lives, and in our quests to live our truths. You may be getting assistance right now - perhaps something you have read has resonated deeply with you. The message I received from this ex-colleague was another in a long series of messages that I had been ignoring. Fortunately, they kept coming and each time with a greater urgency for me to pay attention. I was demonstrating what she wrote about. I was seeking to satisfy my ego and I was struggling with how I thought others perceived me but my endeavour brought me no true fulfilment. I had received instructions to move from where I was and go elsewhere, but I refused to obey. Despite my stubbornness, God's love still continued to pursue me.

I sat in my office that evening and wondered what to do with myself. I wondered where my journey would take me and what was next. I wondered about Mr. Thomas and what he thought of me. I imagined him having a conversation with his wife or a friend concerning what I had done. I also imagined the female associate who was present at the meeting sharing her own opinion.

In the midst of these negative thoughts, I then thought of my higher self and my life's purpose. I felt sure that this is what I had to choose. It was the very thing that was calling me all along. There was an overwhelming realisation that I was not alone on this journey. I felt a sudden burst of comfort and peace. I felt sure about something I could not see and did not know. I did not know where the path would take me, but I decided to be obedient. I was prepared at that point to sell my car and I thought about eventually losing my home if I was unable to make the mortgage payments. As crazy as it may sound, I was prepared to let everything go. I was trusting that no matter what, I would be taken care of.

As I prepared to leave for home that day, I thought, "I guess this is how the ego dies; when we really and truly decide to break free from the opinions of other people."

CHAPTER 8

# *The Place of Surrender*

Mr. Thomas and I had a meeting to discuss what was happening. In the meeting, I told him about my decision to discontinue the law degree programme. I also told him that I had decided to leave the firm and move in another direction. For the first time in a while, I felt properly aligned. There was no part of me that was wrestling with myself. I was not doing something that my mind was against. I was not saying something that my spirit resisted. My mind, body and spirit were in complete alignment and there was no doublemindedness. It felt refreshing to not be afraid of the unknown or what another person thought of me.

Some weeks after the meeting with Mr. Thomas, another paralegal was hired to replace me, and we agreed that I would stay on until December. During that period, I completed my matters and the new person got a chance to train. It was an awkward time. There I was in a job position that I had held for years and someone was waiting to take over from me. I was giving up something that was sure, while being so uncertain of my next move.

There were times when I felt very anxious, but I constantly reminded myself to trust God and His plans for me, even though I did not know what those plans were. I would trust Him, even if I had to leave with no job prospect. I would trust Him, even if it looked like I had no money. I would trust Him, even if it meant losing my house. I would trust Him, even if I had to sell my car. No matter what, I would trust Him.

> Something about total surrender and trust moves God. It is that place where we let go of our wants and needs and say to God, "Let Your will be done."

Something about total surrender and trust moves God. It is that place where we let go of our wants and needs and say to God, "Let Your will be done." With our own desires out of the way, He can show up and do what He wants to do in our lives. It is a scary, but powerful place to be.

CHAPTER 9

# *You Will Know What To Do*

A friend encouraged me to apply for a job at a broadcasting company. I sent in an application, but unfortunately, I was not shortlisted. As December approached, I recall feeling even more anxious, particularly because the time was drawing close when I had to make the transition from my job. One evening, I stayed late at work to complete some tasks. While in my office, I looked up at the ceiling and while staring at the light bulb, I felt inspired to pray. I asked God to tell me what to do. I had surrendered myself completely into His hands and I needed His help, especially since I had dropped everything.

A week after that, I had a dream that would change everything. In the dream, I was in Japan with a group of friends visiting Ally, a former schoolmate. Ally lived in a small room with glass walls that was close to a movie theatre. Everyone had left with her to purchase food, and while they were gone, I decided to explore the neighbourhood.

While walking, I saw some beautiful houses and small islands. I sat on a bench next to a road close to where Ally lived, and a man walked towards me with a bunch of roses. I got the impression that he was going to hand them to me. I wondered who he was and stared at him confused. He laughed and handed the flowers to a woman who was sitting beside me. It turned out that she was his wife and she started laughing with him. I spoke with them for a while and then got up and started walking along the road. As I walked, I saw groups of people laughing and talking, including small children who started playing around me. The atmosphere was buzzing with excitement and that made me feel happy and at home.

A woman from the crowd came up to me and pointed to a place that looked like an island and she said, "That is where Roxanne's sister lives." She was referring to a former schoolmate but later I found this to be interesting because my younger sister's name is also Roxanne. However, I did not make that connection in the dream.

Another woman came up to me and handed me a piece of paper. On the paper she wrote her name and contact numbers and several long email addresses. I asked her what it was for and she said for friendship. She then explained that there was a presence about me that attracted people, things, and nature. I hugged her and told her, "God loves you." It was a loving embrace. I sensed that she was lonely and missed her family, and that she had been away from home for a long time. She asked if I would remember her and I told her that I would. I told her I would remember her as the lady with blonde hair who I had met in the street. I told her other things I would remember about her, like the yellow shirt that she was wearing. She then said something in another language that sounded like "Botswani." She used that word to describe the aura she said was over me. Then, right where we were standing, a small bird began chirping loudly and happily above us. She looked up at it and said, "You see what I mean?" and then she walked away.

I made my way back to Ally's house and the small bird followed me. I noticed it flying and chirping over my head. I paused and looked at it and said, "Botswani! Botswani! I get it!" In that moment, I understood what the woman was trying to say to me earlier.

When I returned to the house, one of my friends was there. I told her I thought we should move to Japan to teach. She immediately disagreed and said she would not go. She told me that Japan was a protected state and if anything should happen, no one from the outside could come into the country to help. She also said that we would experience prejudice. I told her I would go because there was nothing holding me back.

When I woke up that morning, I opened my eyes but did not get out of bed right away. As I laid there thinking about what I had just seen in the dream, I heard something outside my window. It was the sound of a bird chirping. This might sound strange, but it sounded exactly like the bird in the dream that I had had only a short while before. I smiled. At the time, I did not consider that the dream held any prophetic meaning for me, but I remember how happy it made me feel.

I got up and started my daily routine. That morning I walked to my car with an extra pep in my steps. I felt so much joy that I decided to share the dream on Facebook. When I did, a friend of mine commented, "The Lord always has unique ways of talking to you." His comment triggered something in my spirit. I asked myself, "Was that it? Was God giving me directions?" It did not take long for me to realise that He was.

Later that day, I reached out to someone who attended university with me when I did my first

JOURNEY INTO THE UNKNOWN

degree. Her name is Anika and she had posted pictures of Japan on Facebook, so I decided to ask her how she got there. She told me she had applied for a teaching position and two weeks later she sent me the information for a company that was hiring. I applied and after a rigorous interview and application process, I was accepted.

My time at the firm was again extended to January of the following year to handle some additional matters. It was coming to an end and it felt right. My season there was over, and it was time for me to move on to something new. I saw with more clarity that my place of employment had served its purpose. I remembered the young woman who entered the firm and I saw how much I had grown. I was not leaving there the same as when I had started.

> We must be able to accept when one season in our lives is over, otherwise we risk becoming stagnant.

We must be able to accept when one season in our lives is over, otherwise we risk becoming stagnant. We would do ourselves and the world a great disservice, when there is much that we were created for and placed on Earth to accomplish. There are other places for us to see and more people to impact, and we cannot get there if we remain where we are. It is for this reason that our spirits call each of us to take our individual journeys into the unknown.

I ended up selling my car, and the revenue was used to settle outstanding debts. I got a tenant for my house a month before my departure and the rent was enough to cover my mortgage payments. I am surprised at how easily everything worked out to facilitate my departure.

I moved to Japan in March 2018.

Fear and worry are barriers that can prevent us from moving forward, but we must overcome them. When I started the journey, I could not foresee how things would have worked themselves out. I was being asked to climb a whole staircase when I could not see beyond the first step.

This is how God calls us out into the unknown. He hardly ever tells us everything that is in store or how things will develop from one day to the next. All we are asked to do is to take a step and trust Him. This part can be very challenging because it requires so much faith. Even if we are given a glimpse of what is to come through dreams or prophetic ministry, that is all it is - a glimpse. We do not get to see the full picture, and for some of us, that is for our own good.

A friend once shared with me that if we were to see some of the things that we had to go through in order to get to the promises of God, we would tell Him no. It was funny when she said it to me at the time, but her humorous words held much wisdom. The journey into the unknown is not always easy. There are many surprises along the way; some that fill us with laughter, but others that bring us to tears, and at times, regret. If God leads us in a particular direction, we can only trust that it is the right place for us to be.

CHAPTER 10

# *I Finally Got It Right*

It is January 27, 2020 - two years since I resigned as a paralegal. I am now on the floor putting this book together as I was inspired to do. There are things I have learnt from my experiences that I sense God wants me to share with you.

Who would have thought that one day I would get an opportunity to live in one of the biggest cities in the world? I now live in Tokyo by the way. Can you imagine that this is what God was calling me to all along? And only He knows what more is in store.

My apartment is across from a park that has many beautiful trees. They provide me with a sense of calm which help to keep me grounded. It has been a joy to watch the trees lose their leaves and sprout again when the seasons change. Early in the mornings, I can hear birds chirping sweetly on the outside.

Everything around me seems to hold meaning. Even the change in the seasons carry its own message. I have taught many children, from kindergarten to high school, and I have seen the smiling faces, just as I saw them in my dream years ago.

It is amazing to see how much my life has shifted and how much I have grown in such a short time. I have been to places that I never imagined I would go. I still remember being awestruck as I travelled to places like Indonesia, South Korea, Cambodia and Vietnam. These places no longer seem out of my reach. Opportunities that I thought were beyond me are now in close proximity.

I think to myself how different my life could have been today had I allowed fear and the opinions of others regarding my dreams and aspirations to keep me where I was. In those moments of fear and panic, I could not see what was before me. I could not see the glorious plan that God had for my life and the reasons He prompted me to leave where I was.

> Often times, what we think will destroy us are the things that help us to move forward. Many of us have to be shaken up in order to give in to the call of God.

Our difficult life experiences do not come to break us, but to lay the foundation for our elevation. Often times, what we think will destroy us are the things that help us to move forward. Many of us have to be shaken up in order to give in to the call of God. It is only then that He has space to move in our lives.

Maybe you feel prompted to make your own transition from where you are and take your journey into the unknown. Perhaps you feel scared, and like me, you struggle with trying to please others. Maybe this includes your family, friends, people at work or even people within your place of worship. Whoever they are, I have learnt that trying to please people cannot get you where you need to go. In fact it is a recipe for disaster.

There is much joy and peace that comes from being obedient to our inner calling. I would describe this as a deep gut feeling that we were born with that awakens as we grow. Please do not stifle your awakening. Do not continue to ignore the signs and clues that you get. Remember, it is not a coincidence. It is not even a coincidence that you are reading this book right now.

Has it been all rainbows and butterflies since I moved to Japan? Absolutely not. Even now my story is still writing itself and I cannot tell what the next day, weeks or months will hold. Going on the path that is ordained for you does not mean you will not face challenges. But the reward is in knowing that you live in a way that is true to yourself and to God. I would not trade that feeling for anything.

The decisions to leave my job and withdraw from school were not easy. I was so concerned about how people would view me. I thought that I would have to hang my head in shame, but when God began moving in my life, my head was lifted. My soul beamed with joy and my confidence grew. Even some of the people whose criticisms I dreaded began to tell me how proud they were of me and that they too wanted a new beginning.

God will lift your head. Where He wants you is so much better than any place that you may want to remain. There is no shame when you answer the call of God and follow the leading of the Holy Spirit.

My final week at the firm was filled with much peace. It was a peace that passed all understanding and could only have come from God. It is the same peace that I am now feeling as I am getting ready to close this book. That same peace will follow you when you obey God's instructions. It is not always easy at first, as my journey shows, but in the end it is all worth it.

Take that journey into the unknown, my friend. I am excited to see all that awaits you!

*"For I know the plans I have for you, says the Lord, plans to prosper you and not to harm you, plans to give you hope and a future."*

**Jeremiah 29:11 - NIV**

# *Conclusion*

I just took you through my journey from Jamaica to Japan. As you were reading, is there anything that jumped out at you? Is there anything that spoke to a specific area of your life? Look to see. Listen to hear and sense to feel. Did any particular picture come to your mind? Did you hear anything? Did you get a feeling deep within you? I have learnt that these are some of the ways that God speaks to us.

There is power in writing down the things that we hear from God. It is something that I have been doing for years and I am always amazed at how some of the things that I journal manifest in my life, sometimes days, months or years later.

I want you to take some time to reflect and write the things that came to your mind as you read this book.

This is a prayer of encouragement for God's purpose in your life to be fulfiled. I pray that you will have the courage to embark on your own journey. As this is an individualised prayer, I invite you to fill in your name in the blank spaces below.

**Prayer:**

Lord, I thank You for this moment that is orchestrated by You. I thank You that through Your own divine wisdom, You have connected me through this book with _____. I thank You for the power of the Holy Spirit that transcends time, borders, cultures, and languages. I thank You for what You are doing in this moment and for Your sweet still voice that is always speaking to us.

Father, I know that You hear our deepest thoughts. You hear the things that we do not even utter, and You see even the things that we write. I thank You, Lord, that You see the things that were just written, and even if not on paper, I know You see the things that are in _____'s heart. Father, I put these things to You. I stand in agreement with the things that You are being petitioned for. I pray that Your will be done in _____'s life. Lord, in Your own wisdom, You know what to take away from us and what to replace it with.

I thank You, Lord, that everything is being perfected in Your own timing. Remove every fear and worry, Lord. Remove every desire to please others and help _____ to look only to You for approval.

Lord, I thank You for the plans and purposes that You have for _____'s life. There are things that we cannot see, but You know them, You orchestrate them. You know the end from the beginning, so we can trust You.

Amen.

**Personal Prayer:**

*Increase my level of faith in You, oh God. Remind me of the loving caring Father that You are. I pray that in this season Your still small voice will become my greatest friend and as You speak to me concerning my life and my journey, that I will find the courage to move from where I am to where You want me to be. In the name of Jesus Christ, I pray. Amen.*

# About the Author

Sandie Heron works as a language teacher in Tokyo, Japan. She is also a producer and presenter of an inspirational programme on Roots 96.1FM, a radio station in Kingston, Jamaica. Sandie is passionate about hearing the stories of people all over the world and capturing what she calls, "the sweetness of their spirit." She gets excited when she is able to share that sweetness with others. She also enjoys writing, travelling, and meeting new people.

www.ingramcontent.com/pod-product-compliance
Lightning Source LLC
LaVergne TN
LVHW051815080426
835513LV00017B/1963